From the Horse's Mouth

Writers

Emily Thornton Calvo
David Schecter
Paul Seaburn
Lynda Twardowski

new seasons®

"From the day we met,
you had me eating out of your hand!"

Just stallin' for time.

"Slow down, buddy, or next time I'll be back with the cop who was riding me."

Always make time for a little horseplay.

"Next time, either get
a wake-up call or catch
a later train."

"Mommy, I just wanna go
on a merry-go-round."

A quiet moment refreshes the soul.

20

"This Witness Protection Program
isn't all it's cracked up to be."

Who but horse and rider
understand their bond so well?

It's wonderful to know that someone always has your back.

25

"For me, every day is Derby day!"

Before we run, we must walk—
but it's getting up after you fall
that's the hard part.

29

"You mean we can eat as much grass as we want?"

The size of a friend is
no indication of the size of the heart.

"I told him to
bring along a map,
but noooo,
Mr. Big Shot always
knows the way."

"Pucker up, 'cause I'm gonna
plant a wet one on ya!"

There's nothing better than lying on your back and watching the clouds roll by.

Success is often more about
how gracefully one manages the
hurdles than how quickly
one gets to the finish line.

Even on the
coldest days,
love warms us all.

"If you lie down and spread your wings, we can pretend we're Pegasus."

There's nothing like a stable relationship!

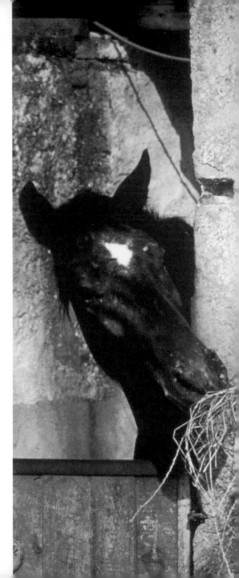

"This is my last triathlon.
After this, I'm sticking
to sprints."

"Just being ne-i-g-h-borly."

"You're right, big fella, this is definitely better than riding in the car with my head out the window."

"There's gotta be grass down here somewhere."

"You're darn right I'm hot to trot!"

"C'mon, tell me the truth:
Does this haircut make
my nose look big?"

"Ever get the feeling
you're going in circles?"

Another thing that
comes in a small package:
A close friend.

64

Dare to go against the crowd.

"Waiter, I'd like another one of those, and a few carrots for dessert."

"One more chorus
of 'Over the River
and Thru the Wood,'
and I'm heading
for home."

"This isn't what I had in mind when I said I wanted a red convertible."

"You scratch my back,
and I'll scratch yours."

"Are we there yet?"

Best friends always share.